50 Breakfast Sandwiches You Need to Try

By: Kelly Johnson

Table of Contents

- Classic Bacon, Egg, and Cheese
- Avocado, Egg, and Spinach on Whole Wheat
- Sausage, Egg, and Cheddar on a Biscuit
- Smoked Salmon and Cream Cheese on a Bagel
- Ham, Egg, and Swiss on a Croissant
- Veggie Scramble with Feta on Toast
- Turkey Bacon, Egg, and Tomato on a Muffin
- Breakfast Burrito with Egg and Salsa
- Chorizo, Egg, and Cheese on a Bun
- Grilled Cheese with Scrambled Egg and Bacon
- Egg and Sausage on a Brioche Bun
- Huevos Rancheros on a Tortilla
- Classic Bacon, Egg, and Avocado on Sourdough
- Sweet Potato and Egg on an English Muffin
- Egg and Mushroom on Rye
- Tofu Scramble with Avocado on Whole Wheat
- Pulled Pork, Egg, and BBQ Sauce on a Roll
- Steak and Egg on an Onion Roll
- Chicken Sausage, Egg, and Swiss on a Bagel
- Pesto and Egg on a Croissant
- Spicy Jalapeño, Egg, and Cheddar on a Biscuit
- Egg and Avocado on Multigrain Bread
- Poached Egg, Spinach, and Tomato on a Roll
- Bacon, Egg, and Brie on a French Baguette
- Smoked Turkey, Egg, and Havarti on Rye
- Veggie and Hummus Egg Sandwich
- Grilled Portobello Mushroom and Egg on Ciabatta
- Egg and Bacon with Chipotle Mayo on a Bagel
- Falafel and Scrambled Eggs on a Pita
- Smashed Avocado, Egg, and Tomato on a Toasted Bagel
- Grilled Chicken, Egg, and Pesto on a Brioche Bun
- Egg, Arugula, and Prosciutto on Sourdough
- BBQ Egg and Bacon Sandwich
- Egg, Tomato, and Basil on Ciabatta
- Sausage, Egg, and Apple Chutney on a Muffin

- Egg and Guacamole on a Toasted Bun
- Roasted Pepper, Egg, and Mozzarella on a Bagel
- Scrambled Eggs with Peppers and Cheese on a Wrap
- Egg and Cheddar with a Dill Pickle on Rye
- Smoked Salmon, Egg, and Cream Cheese on a Bagel
- Egg, Bacon, and Chipotle Mayo on a Croissant
- Grilled Veggie and Egg Sandwich
- Egg and Pimento Cheese on Biscuit
- Sausage, Egg, and Avocado on Whole Wheat
- Avocado, Spinach, and Egg on Rye
- BLT with Egg on a Toasted Bun
- Egg and Arugula with Parmesan on Sourdough
- Chive Scrambled Egg and Swiss on a Roll
- Egg, Kale, and Cheddar on a Toasted Bagel
- Pork Belly, Egg, and Spicy Aioli on a Croissant

Classic Bacon, Egg, and Cheese

Ingredients:

- 2 slices bacon
- 1 egg
- 1 English muffin, split
- 1 slice cheddar cheese
- Butter, for toasting

Instructions:

1. **Cook bacon** – Fry bacon in a pan over medium heat until crispy, then remove and drain on paper towels.
2. **Cook egg** – In the same pan, fry egg to your preferred doneness (scrambled or sunny side up).
3. **Toast muffin** – Butter the English muffin and toast it in the pan until golden brown.
4. **Assemble sandwich** – Place the cheese slice on the bottom half of the muffin, followed by the egg, bacon, and top half of the muffin.
5. **Serve** – Enjoy your classic breakfast sandwich warm!

Avocado, Egg, and Spinach on Whole Wheat

Ingredients:

- 1 egg
- 1/2 avocado, sliced
- 1 cup spinach
- 1 slice whole wheat bread
- Olive oil, for sautéing
- Salt and pepper, to taste

Instructions:

1. **Cook egg** – Fry egg to your preferred doneness.
2. **Sauté spinach** – Sauté spinach in a bit of olive oil until wilted. Season with salt and pepper.
3. **Toast bread** – Toast the whole wheat bread to your liking.
4. **Assemble** – Place avocado slices on the toasted bread, top with sautéed spinach and the fried egg.
5. **Serve** – Serve immediately for a healthy and filling breakfast.

Sausage, Egg, and Cheddar on a Biscuit

Ingredients:

- 1 sausage patty
- 1 egg
- 1 cheddar cheese slice
- 1 biscuit (store-bought or homemade)

Instructions:

1. **Cook sausage** – Fry the sausage patty in a pan until browned and cooked through.
2. **Cook egg** – In the same pan, fry the egg to your desired doneness.
3. **Toast biscuit** – Split and toast the biscuit lightly in a pan.
4. **Assemble sandwich** – Place the sausage patty on the bottom half of the biscuit, then top with the fried egg and cheddar cheese.
5. **Serve** – Enjoy this warm and hearty breakfast sandwich!

Smoked Salmon and Cream Cheese on a Bagel

Ingredients:

- 1 bagel, split
- 2 oz smoked salmon
- 2 tbsp cream cheese
- 1 tsp capers (optional)
- Fresh dill, for garnish

Instructions:

1. **Toast bagel** – Split and toast the bagel until golden brown.
2. **Spread cream cheese** – Spread cream cheese generously on each half of the bagel.
3. **Assemble** – Top with smoked salmon, capers (if using), and fresh dill.
4. **Serve** – Serve immediately for a light yet flavorful breakfast or brunch.

Ham, Egg, and Swiss on a Croissant

Ingredients:

- 1 egg
- 2 slices ham
- 1 slice Swiss cheese
- 1 croissant, sliced in half
- Butter, for toasting

Instructions:

1. **Cook egg** – Fry egg to your preferred doneness.
2. **Toast croissant** – Butter the croissant and toast it in a pan until golden brown.
3. **Assemble sandwich** – Place the ham slices on the bottom half of the croissant, followed by the egg and Swiss cheese.
4. **Serve** – Enjoy your delicious croissant sandwich immediately!

Veggie Scramble with Feta on Toast

Ingredients:

- 2 eggs
- 1/4 cup feta cheese, crumbled
- 1/4 cup bell pepper, chopped
- 1/4 cup onion, chopped
- 1/4 cup spinach, chopped
- 1 slice whole grain bread
- Olive oil, for sautéing

Instructions:

1. **Sauté veggies** – In a pan, sauté bell pepper, onion, and spinach in a little olive oil until softened.
2. **Scramble eggs** – In a bowl, whisk the eggs and pour them into the pan with the veggies. Scramble until cooked through.
3. **Toast bread** – Toast a slice of whole grain bread.
4. **Assemble** – Place the veggie scramble on top of the toasted bread, and sprinkle with crumbled feta cheese.
5. **Serve** – Serve warm for a delicious veggie-packed breakfast.

Turkey Bacon, Egg, and Tomato on a Muffin

Ingredients:

- 2 slices turkey bacon
- 1 egg
- 1 tomato, sliced
- 1 English muffin, split
- Butter, for toasting

Instructions:

1. **Cook bacon** – Fry turkey bacon in a pan over medium heat until crispy, then remove and set aside.
2. **Cook egg** – In the same pan, fry egg to your preferred doneness.
3. **Toast muffin** – Butter and toast the English muffin.
4. **Assemble sandwich** – Place the fried egg, crispy bacon, and tomato slices on the bottom half of the muffin.
5. **Serve** – Enjoy your light and tasty breakfast sandwich.

Breakfast Burrito with Egg and Salsa

Ingredients:

- 2 eggs, scrambled
- 1 flour tortilla
- ¼ cup salsa
- 1/4 cup shredded cheese (optional)
- 1 tbsp olive oil (optional)

Instructions:

1. **Cook eggs** – Scramble eggs in a pan over medium heat, adding a bit of olive oil if desired.
2. **Warm tortilla** – Heat the tortilla in a pan for 1–2 minutes on each side.
3. **Assemble burrito** – Spread scrambled eggs on the tortilla, top with salsa and cheese (if using).
4. **Roll up** – Fold the sides of the tortilla in and roll it up tightly.
5. **Serve** – Serve immediately for a delicious, handheld breakfast.

Chorizo, Egg, and Cheese on a Bun

Ingredients:

- 1/2 lb chorizo sausage
- 2 eggs
- 1/4 cup cheddar cheese, shredded
- 1 sandwich bun

Instructions:

1. **Cook chorizo** – In a pan, cook the chorizo over medium heat, breaking it up into crumbles as it cooks.
2. **Cook eggs** – In the same pan, scramble the eggs and cook until just set.
3. **Assemble sandwich** – Place the chorizo and egg mixture on the sandwich bun, then sprinkle with shredded cheese.
4. **Serve** – Serve immediately for a spicy, savory breakfast sandwich.

Grilled Cheese with Scrambled Egg and Bacon

Ingredients:

- 2 slices bread (sourdough or white)
- 2 slices bacon
- 2 eggs
- 1 tbsp butter
- 2 slices cheddar cheese

Instructions:

1. **Cook bacon** – Fry bacon in a pan over medium heat until crispy, then drain on paper towels.
2. **Scramble eggs** – In a bowl, whisk eggs, then scramble them in the same pan. Remove from heat.
3. **Assemble sandwich** – Butter one side of each bread slice. On the unbuttered side, layer one slice of cheese, scrambled eggs, bacon, and another slice of cheese.
4. **Grill** – Cook sandwich in a pan over medium heat until golden brown on both sides and the cheese is melted.
5. **Serve** – Slice and enjoy warm.

Egg and Sausage on a Brioche Bun

Ingredients:

- 1 sausage patty
- 1 egg
- 1 brioche bun, split
- 1 slice cheddar cheese
- Butter, for toasting

Instructions:

1. **Cook sausage** – Fry the sausage patty in a pan over medium heat until browned and cooked through.
2. **Cook egg** – Fry egg to your desired doneness.
3. **Toast bun** – Butter the brioche bun and lightly toast in a pan.
4. **Assemble sandwich** – Place the sausage patty, egg, and cheese inside the bun.
5. **Serve** – Serve warm for a delicious, fluffy breakfast sandwich.

Huevos Rancheros on a Tortilla

Ingredients:

- 2 eggs
- 1 small flour or corn tortilla
- ½ cup refried beans
- ½ cup salsa
- ¼ cup shredded cheese (cheddar or cotija)
- Fresh cilantro, for garnish

Instructions:

1. **Warm tortilla** – Heat tortilla in a pan or oven until slightly crispy.
2. **Cook eggs** – Fry eggs to your preferred doneness.
3. **Assemble** – Spread refried beans over the tortilla, top with eggs, salsa, and shredded cheese.
4. **Serve** – Garnish with fresh cilantro and enjoy!

Classic Bacon, Egg, and Avocado on Sourdough

Ingredients:

- 2 slices sourdough bread
- 2 slices bacon
- 1 egg
- ½ avocado, mashed
- 1 tbsp butter

Instructions:

1. **Cook bacon** – Fry bacon until crispy and set aside.
2. **Cook egg** – Fry egg to your desired doneness.
3. **Toast bread** – Butter and toast sourdough slices in a pan.
4. **Assemble** – Spread mashed avocado on toasted sourdough, add the egg, then bacon.
5. **Serve** – Enjoy as an open-faced or sandwich-style breakfast.

Sweet Potato and Egg on an English Muffin

Ingredients:

- 1 English muffin, split
- 1 small sweet potato, roasted and mashed
- 1 egg
- 1 tbsp olive oil
- Salt and pepper, to taste

Instructions:

1. **Roast sweet potato** – Mash a previously roasted sweet potato with salt and pepper.
2. **Cook egg** – Fry egg in a pan with olive oil.
3. **Toast muffin** – Toast English muffin until golden brown.
4. **Assemble** – Spread mashed sweet potato on one half, add the fried egg, and top with the other muffin half.
5. **Serve** – Serve warm for a nutritious start to the day.

Egg and Mushroom on Rye

Ingredients:

- 2 slices rye bread
- 1 egg
- ½ cup mushrooms, sliced
- 1 tbsp butter
- 1 tbsp cream cheese (optional)

Instructions:

1. **Sauté mushrooms** – In a pan, cook mushrooms with butter until soft and golden brown.
2. **Cook egg** – Fry or scramble the egg in the same pan.
3. **Toast rye bread** – Toast rye slices and spread with cream cheese if using.
4. **Assemble** – Layer mushrooms and egg on one slice, then top with the other slice of bread.
5. **Serve** – Serve immediately.

Tofu Scramble with Avocado on Whole Wheat

Ingredients:

- ½ block firm tofu, crumbled
- ½ avocado, sliced
- 1 tbsp olive oil
- ¼ tsp turmeric
- ¼ tsp garlic powder
- Salt and pepper, to taste
- 1 slice whole wheat bread

Instructions:

1. **Cook tofu** – Heat olive oil in a pan, then sauté crumbled tofu with turmeric, garlic powder, salt, and pepper for 5 minutes.
2. **Toast bread** – Toast whole wheat bread.
3. **Assemble** – Spread tofu scramble over toast and top with sliced avocado.
4. **Serve** – Serve warm as a hearty plant-based breakfast.

Pulled Pork, Egg, and BBQ Sauce on a Roll

Ingredients:

- ½ cup pulled pork
- 1 egg
- 1 tbsp BBQ sauce
- 1 sandwich roll

Instructions:

1. **Heat pulled pork** – Warm pulled pork in a pan or microwave.
2. **Cook egg** – Fry egg in a pan to your liking.
3. **Toast roll** – Lightly toast sandwich roll.
4. **Assemble** – Spread BBQ sauce on the roll, add pulled pork and egg.
5. **Serve** – Serve warm for a flavorful breakfast sandwich.

Steak and Egg on an Onion Roll

Ingredients:

- 1 small steak (sirloin or ribeye)
- 1 egg
- 1 onion roll, split
- 1 tbsp butter
- Salt and pepper, to taste

Instructions:

1. **Cook steak** – Season steak with salt and pepper, then grill or pan-sear for 3–4 minutes per side. Let rest and slice thinly.
2. **Cook egg** – Fry egg in butter to your preferred doneness.
3. **Toast roll** – Toast the onion roll until slightly crispy.
4. **Assemble** – Place sliced steak and egg inside the roll.
5. **Serve** – Serve warm with extra seasoning if desired.

Chicken Sausage, Egg, and Swiss on a Bagel

Ingredients:

- 1 chicken sausage patty
- 1 egg
- 1 slice Swiss cheese
- 1 bagel, split
- Butter, for toasting

Instructions:

1. **Cook sausage** – Fry chicken sausage patty until golden brown and cooked through.
2. **Cook egg** – Fry egg to desired doneness.
3. **Toast bagel** – Butter and toast bagel halves.
4. **Assemble** – Layer Swiss cheese, sausage, and egg inside the bagel.
5. **Serve** – Serve warm for a hearty breakfast sandwich.

Pesto and Egg on a Croissant

Ingredients:

- 1 croissant, sliced in half
- 1 egg
- 1 tbsp pesto
- 1 slice mozzarella or provolone cheese
- Butter, for toasting

Instructions:

1. **Cook egg** – Fry or scramble the egg to your preferred doneness.
2. **Toast croissant** – Lightly butter and toast the croissant in a pan.
3. **Assemble** – Spread pesto on the croissant, add the egg, and top with cheese.
4. **Serve** – Serve warm and enjoy this buttery, flavorful sandwich.

Spicy Jalapeño, Egg, and Cheddar on a Biscuit

Ingredients:

- 1 biscuit (store-bought or homemade)
- 1 egg
- 2 tbsp shredded cheddar cheese
- 1 jalapeño, sliced
- 1 tbsp butter

Instructions:

1. **Cook egg** – Scramble or fry the egg to your liking.
2. **Sauté jalapeños** – In a pan, lightly sauté jalapeño slices with butter until slightly softened.
3. **Toast biscuit** – Split and toast the biscuit.
4. **Assemble** – Place egg, sautéed jalapeños, and shredded cheddar on the biscuit.
5. **Serve** – Serve warm with a side of hot sauce for extra heat.

Egg and Avocado on Multigrain Bread

Ingredients:

- 1 slice multigrain bread, toasted
- 1 egg
- ½ avocado, mashed
- 1 tsp lemon juice
- Salt and pepper, to taste

Instructions:

1. **Cook egg** – Fry, poach, or scramble the egg.
2. **Prepare avocado** – Mash avocado with lemon juice, salt, and pepper.
3. **Assemble** – Spread mashed avocado on toasted multigrain bread, top with the cooked egg.
4. **Serve** – Enjoy open-faced or add another slice of bread for a sandwich.

Poached Egg, Spinach, and Tomato on a Roll

Ingredients:

- 1 small sandwich roll
- 1 egg
- ½ cup fresh spinach
- 1 tomato slice
- 1 tbsp olive oil
- Salt and pepper, to taste

Instructions:

1. **Poach egg** – Bring water to a simmer, crack in the egg, and cook for 3–4 minutes.
2. **Sauté spinach** – Sauté spinach in olive oil until wilted.
3. **Toast roll** – Slice and lightly toast the sandwich roll.
4. **Assemble** – Layer spinach, tomato, and poached egg on the roll.
5. **Serve** – Season with salt and pepper, then enjoy.

Bacon, Egg, and Brie on a French Baguette

Ingredients:

- 1 small French baguette, sliced open
- 2 slices bacon
- 1 egg
- 2 slices Brie cheese
- 1 tbsp butter

Instructions:

1. **Cook bacon** – Fry bacon until crispy, then drain on paper towels.
2. **Cook egg** – Fry the egg to your preferred doneness.
3. **Toast baguette** – Lightly toast baguette slices in butter.
4. **Assemble** – Layer Brie cheese, bacon, and egg inside the baguette.
5. **Serve** – Serve warm with a side of fruit or coffee.

Smoked Turkey, Egg, and Havarti on Rye

Ingredients:

- 2 slices rye bread
- 1 egg
- 2 slices smoked turkey
- 1 slice Havarti cheese
- 1 tbsp butter

Instructions:

1. **Cook egg** – Fry the egg to your preferred doneness.
2. **Toast rye bread** – Lightly butter and toast the rye bread in a pan.
3. **Assemble** – Place turkey slices, egg, and Havarti cheese between the toasted rye slices.
4. **Serve** – Serve warm for a savory, smoky breakfast sandwich.

Veggie and Hummus Egg Sandwich

Ingredients:

- 1 whole wheat sandwich roll
- 1 egg
- 2 tbsp hummus
- ¼ cup shredded carrots
- ¼ cup cucumber slices
- 1 tbsp olive oil
- Salt and pepper, to taste

Instructions:

1. **Cook egg** – Scramble or fry the egg.
2. **Toast roll** – Lightly toast the sandwich roll.
3. **Assemble** – Spread hummus on one half of the roll, add shredded carrots, cucumber, and the cooked egg.
4. **Serve** – Serve warm or chilled for a light, veggie-packed meal.

Grilled Portobello Mushroom and Egg on Ciabatta

Ingredients:

- 1 ciabatta roll, sliced
- 1 large Portobello mushroom cap
- 1 egg
- 1 tbsp olive oil
- 1 tsp balsamic vinegar
- Salt and pepper, to taste

Instructions:

1. **Grill mushroom** – Brush the Portobello with olive oil and balsamic vinegar, then grill or pan-fry for 5–7 minutes per side.
2. **Cook egg** – Fry the egg in a pan until set.
3. **Toast ciabatta** – Lightly toast the ciabatta roll.
4. **Assemble** – Layer the mushroom and egg inside the roll.
5. **Serve** – Serve warm with a side salad or roasted potatoes.

Egg and Bacon with Chipotle Mayo on a Bagel

Ingredients:

- 1 bagel, split
- 2 slices bacon
- 1 egg
- 1 tbsp chipotle mayo
- Butter, for toasting

Instructions:

1. **Cook bacon** – Fry bacon until crispy.
2. **Cook egg** – Fry egg to desired doneness.
3. **Toast bagel** – Butter and toast the bagel until golden brown.
4. **Assemble** – Spread chipotle mayo on one half of the bagel, add bacon and egg, then top with the other half.
5. **Serve** – Enjoy warm for a smoky, spicy breakfast sandwich.

Falafel and Scrambled Eggs on a Pita

Ingredients:

- 3 small falafels, warmed
- 2 eggs, scrambled
- 1 whole wheat pita, halved
- 2 tbsp hummus
- 1 tbsp tahini (optional)
- Fresh parsley, for garnish

Instructions:

1. **Warm falafels** – Heat falafels in a pan or microwave until warm.
2. **Scramble eggs** – Cook eggs in a pan over medium heat until soft and fluffy.
3. **Assemble pita** – Spread hummus inside the pita halves, then stuff with scrambled eggs and falafels.
4. **Serve** – Drizzle with tahini and garnish with fresh parsley.

Smashed Avocado, Egg, and Tomato on a Toasted Bagel

Ingredients:

- 1 bagel, split and toasted
- 1 egg
- ½ avocado, mashed
- 1 tomato, sliced
- 1 tsp lemon juice
- Salt and pepper, to taste

Instructions:

1. **Cook egg** – Fry or poach the egg.
2. **Prepare avocado** – Mash avocado with lemon juice, salt, and pepper.
3. **Assemble sandwich** – Spread avocado on the toasted bagel, layer tomato slices, and top with the cooked egg.
4. **Serve** – Serve warm with an extra sprinkle of salt and pepper.

Grilled Chicken, Egg, and Pesto on a Brioche Bun

Ingredients:

- 1 grilled chicken breast, sliced
- 1 egg
- 1 brioche bun, split
- 1 tbsp pesto
- 1 slice mozzarella cheese

Instructions:

1. **Cook egg** – Fry egg to your desired doneness.
2. **Toast bun** – Lightly toast brioche bun in a pan.
3. **Assemble** – Spread pesto on the bottom bun, add grilled chicken, mozzarella, and fried egg.
4. **Serve** – Enjoy warm for a satisfying breakfast sandwich.

Egg, Arugula, and Prosciutto on Sourdough

Ingredients:

- 2 slices sourdough bread, toasted
- 1 egg
- 2 slices prosciutto
- ½ cup arugula
- 1 tbsp olive oil
- Salt and pepper, to taste

Instructions:

1. **Cook egg** – Fry egg to your preferred doneness.
2. **Toast sourdough** – Lightly toast bread slices.
3. **Assemble sandwich** – Layer arugula, prosciutto, and egg on one slice of sourdough.
4. **Serve** – Drizzle with olive oil, season with salt and pepper, and enjoy.

BBQ Egg and Bacon Sandwich

Ingredients:

- 1 sandwich roll, split
- 2 slices bacon
- 1 egg
- 1 tbsp BBQ sauce
- Butter, for toasting

Instructions:

1. **Cook bacon** – Fry until crispy, then set aside.
2. **Cook egg** – Fry egg to your desired doneness.
3. **Toast roll** – Butter and lightly toast sandwich roll.
4. **Assemble sandwich** – Spread BBQ sauce on the roll, add bacon and egg.
5. **Serve** – Serve warm with extra BBQ sauce if desired.

Egg, Tomato, and Basil on Ciabatta

Ingredients:

- 1 ciabatta roll, split
- 1 egg
- 1 tomato, sliced
- 2 fresh basil leaves
- 1 tbsp olive oil
- Salt and pepper, to taste

Instructions:

1. **Cook egg** – Fry egg in a pan with olive oil.
2. **Toast ciabatta** – Lightly toast ciabatta roll.
3. **Assemble sandwich** – Layer tomato slices, basil leaves, and the egg inside the roll.
4. **Serve** – Season with salt and pepper and serve warm.

Sausage, Egg, and Apple Chutney on a Muffin

Ingredients:

- 1 English muffin, split and toasted
- 1 sausage patty
- 1 egg
- 2 tbsp apple chutney

Instructions:

1. **Cook sausage** – Fry sausage patty until browned and fully cooked.
2. **Cook egg** – Fry or scramble egg.
3. **Toast muffin** – Toast English muffin until golden brown.
4. **Assemble sandwich** – Spread apple chutney on one side of the muffin, then add sausage and egg.
5. **Serve** – Enjoy warm for a sweet and savory combination.

Egg and Guacamole on a Toasted Bun

Ingredients:

- 1 sandwich bun, toasted
- 1 egg
- 2 tbsp guacamole
- 1 tsp lime juice
- Salt and pepper, to taste

Instructions:

1. **Cook egg** – Fry egg to your preferred doneness.
2. **Prepare guacamole** – If making fresh, mash avocado with lime juice, salt, and pepper.
3. **Toast bun** – Lightly toast sandwich bun.
4. **Assemble sandwich** – Spread guacamole on the bottom bun, top with the fried egg.
5. **Serve** – Serve immediately for a creamy, flavorful breakfast.

Roasted Pepper, Egg, and Mozzarella on a Bagel

Ingredients:

- 1 bagel, split and toasted
- 1 egg
- ½ roasted red bell pepper, sliced
- 1 slice mozzarella cheese
- 1 tbsp olive oil

Instructions:

1. **Roast pepper** – If not pre-roasted, char a red bell pepper under the broiler for 5–7 minutes, then slice.
2. **Cook egg** – Fry or scramble egg.
3. **Toast bagel** – Lightly toast the bagel.
4. **Assemble sandwich** – Layer roasted red pepper, mozzarella, and egg inside the bagel.
5. **Serve** – Serve warm with an extra drizzle of olive oil.

Scrambled Eggs with Peppers and Cheese on a Wrap

Ingredients:

- 2 eggs
- ¼ cup bell peppers, diced (red, green, or yellow)
- ¼ cup shredded cheddar cheese
- 1 tortilla wrap
- 1 tbsp butter or olive oil
- Salt and pepper, to taste

Instructions:

1. **Sauté peppers** – Heat butter or olive oil in a pan and sauté diced peppers until soft.
2. **Scramble eggs** – Add whisked eggs to the pan, season with salt and pepper, and cook until fluffy.
3. **Assemble wrap** – Place scrambled eggs and sautéed peppers on the tortilla, sprinkle with cheese, and roll up tightly.
4. **Serve** – Serve warm, cut in half if desired.

Egg and Cheddar with a Dill Pickle on Rye

Ingredients:

- 2 slices rye bread
- 1 egg
- 1 slice cheddar cheese
- 2 dill pickle slices
- 1 tbsp butter

Instructions:

1. **Cook egg** – Fry egg to your preferred doneness.
2. **Toast bread** – Butter and lightly toast rye bread in a pan.
3. **Assemble sandwich** – Place cheddar cheese on one slice, followed by the fried egg and dill pickle slices. Top with the second slice of rye bread.
4. **Serve** – Serve warm with an extra pickle on the side.

Smoked Salmon, Egg, and Cream Cheese on a Bagel

Ingredients:

- 1 bagel, split and toasted
- 1 egg, soft scrambled or fried
- 2 oz smoked salmon
- 2 tbsp cream cheese
- 1 tsp capers (optional)
- Fresh dill, for garnish

Instructions:

1. **Prepare egg** – Soft scramble or fry the egg.
2. **Toast bagel** – Toast bagel until golden brown.
3. **Assemble sandwich** – Spread cream cheese on each bagel half, layer smoked salmon and egg, and sprinkle with capers if using.
4. **Serve** – Garnish with fresh dill and serve warm.

Egg, Bacon, and Chipotle Mayo on a Croissant

Ingredients:

- 1 croissant, sliced in half
- 1 egg
- 2 slices bacon
- 1 tbsp chipotle mayo
- 1 tbsp butter

Instructions:

1. **Cook bacon** – Fry bacon until crispy, then set aside.
2. **Cook egg** – Fry egg to your preferred doneness.
3. **Toast croissant** – Butter and lightly toast croissant halves in a pan.
4. **Assemble sandwich** – Spread chipotle mayo on the croissant, then layer bacon and egg inside.
5. **Serve** – Serve warm and enjoy this smoky, buttery sandwich.

Grilled Veggie and Egg Sandwich

Ingredients:

- 2 slices whole wheat or ciabatta bread
- 1 egg
- ¼ cup zucchini, sliced
- ¼ cup bell pepper, sliced
- 1 tbsp olive oil
- 1 slice provolone or mozzarella cheese
- Salt and pepper, to taste

Instructions:

1. **Grill vegetables** – Heat olive oil in a pan and grill zucchini and bell pepper slices until tender.
2. **Cook egg** – Fry egg to desired doneness.
3. **Toast bread** – Lightly toast bread slices in a pan.
4. **Assemble sandwich** – Place grilled veggies and cheese on one slice, add egg, and top with the second slice of bread.
5. **Serve** – Serve warm as a hearty, veggie-packed breakfast.

Egg and Pimento Cheese on a Biscuit

Ingredients:

- 1 biscuit (store-bought or homemade)
- 1 egg
- 2 tbsp pimento cheese
- 1 tbsp butter

Instructions:

1. **Cook egg** – Scramble or fry egg to your preference.
2. **Toast biscuit** – Slice biscuit in half and toast lightly in a pan with butter.
3. **Assemble sandwich** – Spread pimento cheese on the bottom half, add egg, and top with the other biscuit half.
4. **Serve** – Serve warm for a rich and cheesy Southern-style breakfast.

Sausage, Egg, and Avocado on Whole Wheat

Ingredients:

- 1 whole wheat sandwich roll
- 1 sausage patty
- 1 egg
- ½ avocado, mashed
- 1 tsp lemon juice
- Salt and pepper, to taste

Instructions:

1. **Cook sausage** – Fry sausage patty in a pan until browned and cooked through.
2. **Cook egg** – Fry egg to desired doneness.
3. **Prepare avocado** – Mash avocado with lemon juice, salt, and pepper.
4. **Toast roll** – Lightly toast the whole wheat roll.
5. **Assemble sandwich** – Spread mashed avocado on the roll, then layer the sausage patty and egg.
6. **Serve** – Serve warm for a hearty and nutritious breakfast.

Avocado, Spinach, and Egg on Rye

Ingredients:

- 2 slices rye bread
- 1 egg
- ½ avocado, mashed
- ½ cup fresh spinach
- 1 tbsp olive oil
- Salt and pepper, to taste

Instructions:

1. **Cook egg** – Fry or poach the egg.
2. **Sauté spinach** – Heat olive oil in a pan and sauté spinach until wilted.
3. **Toast rye bread** – Toast the rye slices until golden.
4. **Assemble** – Spread mashed avocado on one slice, add sautéed spinach and egg, and top with the other slice.
5. **Serve** – Serve immediately for a nutrient-packed breakfast.

BLT with Egg on a Toasted Bun

Ingredients:

- 1 sandwich bun, toasted
- 2 slices bacon
- 1 egg
- 2 lettuce leaves
- 2 tomato slices
- 1 tbsp mayonnaise

Instructions:

1. **Cook bacon** – Fry until crispy, then drain on paper towels.
2. **Cook egg** – Fry egg to preferred doneness.
3. **Toast bun** – Lightly toast sandwich bun.
4. **Assemble sandwich** – Spread mayonnaise on one side of the bun, then layer lettuce, tomato, bacon, and egg.
5. **Serve** – Serve warm with a side of fruit or hash browns.

Egg and Arugula with Parmesan on Sourdough

Ingredients:

- 2 slices sourdough bread
- 1 egg
- ½ cup arugula
- 2 tbsp shaved Parmesan cheese
- 1 tbsp olive oil
- Salt and pepper, to taste

Instructions:

1. **Cook egg** – Fry or poach the egg.
2. **Toast bread** – Lightly toast sourdough slices.
3. **Assemble** – Layer arugula and Parmesan on one slice of toast, add egg, and top with the second slice.
4. **Serve** – Drizzle with olive oil and season with salt and pepper.

Chive Scrambled Egg and Swiss on a Roll

Ingredients:

- 1 sandwich roll
- 2 eggs
- 1 tbsp fresh chives, chopped
- 1 slice Swiss cheese
- 1 tbsp butter
- Salt and pepper, to taste

Instructions:

1. **Scramble eggs** – In a bowl, whisk eggs, chives, salt, and pepper. Scramble in a pan with butter until fluffy.
2. **Toast roll** – Slice and lightly toast the sandwich roll.
3. **Assemble sandwich** – Place scrambled eggs inside the roll and top with Swiss cheese.
4. **Serve** – Serve warm with a side of fresh fruit.

Egg, Kale, and Cheddar on a Toasted Bagel

Ingredients:

- 1 bagel, split and toasted
- 1 egg
- ½ cup kale, chopped
- 1 slice cheddar cheese
- 1 tbsp olive oil
- Salt and pepper, to taste

Instructions:

1. **Cook egg** – Fry or scramble egg.
2. **Sauté kale** – Heat olive oil in a pan and sauté kale until wilted.
3. **Toast bagel** – Lightly toast bagel halves.
4. **Assemble sandwich** – Place cheddar cheese, kale, and egg inside the bagel.
5. **Serve** – Serve warm with your favorite breakfast beverage.

Pork Belly, Egg, and Spicy Aioli on a Croissant

Ingredients:

- 1 croissant, sliced in half
- 1 slice pork belly (or thick-cut bacon)
- 1 egg
- 1 tbsp spicy aioli (mayonnaise + sriracha)
- 1 tbsp butter

Instructions:

1. **Cook pork belly** – Pan-fry pork belly until crispy on the edges.
2. **Cook egg** – Fry egg to desired doneness.
3. **Toast croissant** – Lightly butter and toast croissant halves.
4. **Assemble sandwich** – Spread spicy aioli on the croissant, then layer pork belly and egg.
5. **Serve** – Serve warm for an indulgent, flavorful breakfast sandwich.